Little Feet

WRITTEN BY
Deborah Wagner Brenneman

ILLUSTRATED BY
Kristina Bender

WestBow Press books may be ordered through booksellers or by contacting:

WestBow Press
A Division of Thomas Nelson & Zondervan
1663 Liberty Drive
Bloomington, IN 47403
www.westbowpress.com
844-714-3454

• Scripture quotation is taken from the Holy Bible, NEW INTERNATIONAL VERSION®, NIV® Copyright © 1973, 1978, 1984, 2011 by Biblica, Inc.® Used by permission. All rights reserved worldwide.

Interior Image Credit: Kristina Bender

ISBN: 979-8-3850-0624-3 (sc)
ISBN: 979-8-3850-0626-7 (hc)
ISBN: 979-8-3850-0625-0 (e)

Library of Congress Control Number: 2023916405

Print information available on the last page.

WestBow Press rev. date: 09/27/2023

Dedication

Deborah-To my beautiful granddaughters! Nana loves you so much! You have inspired me to write this book from watching you grow right before my eyes. May you always give praise to our creator, and live your life for Jesus Christ.

Kristina-To Hallie and the little one we can't wait to meet!

Matthew 19:14 Jesus said, "Let the little children come to me, and do not hinder them, for the kingdom of heaven belongs to such as these."

"Anyone who welcomes a little child like this on my behalf welcomes me, and anyone who welcomes me welcomes not only me but also my Father who sent me." -Mark 9:37 NLT

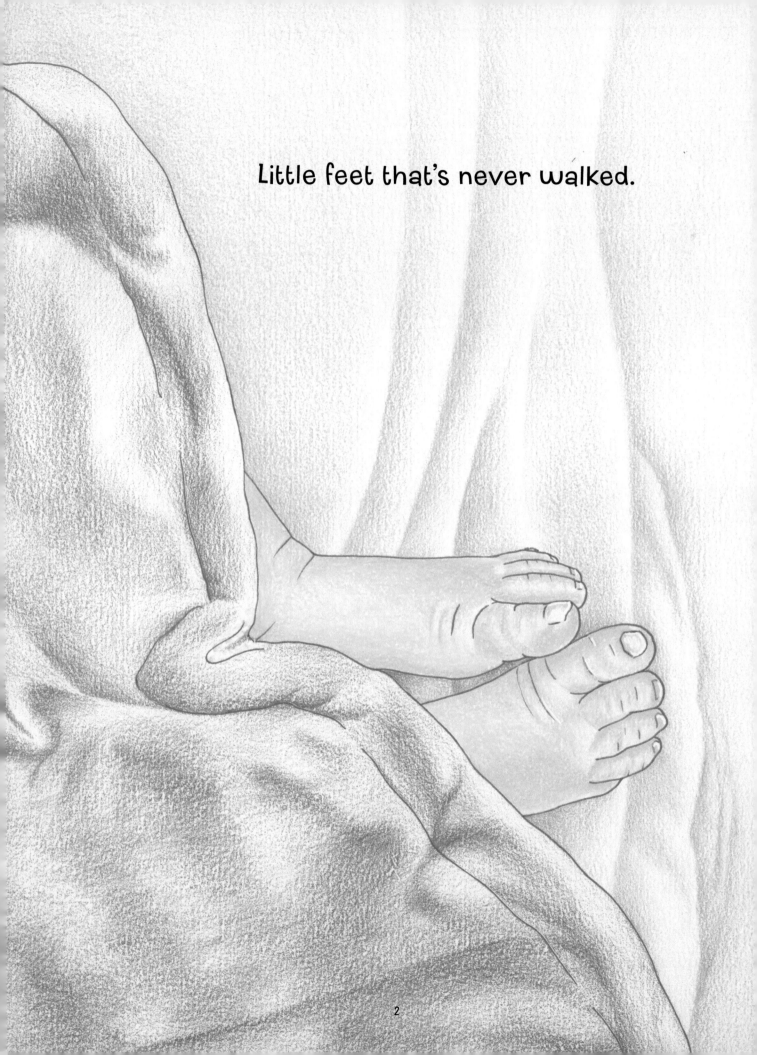

Little feet that's never walked.

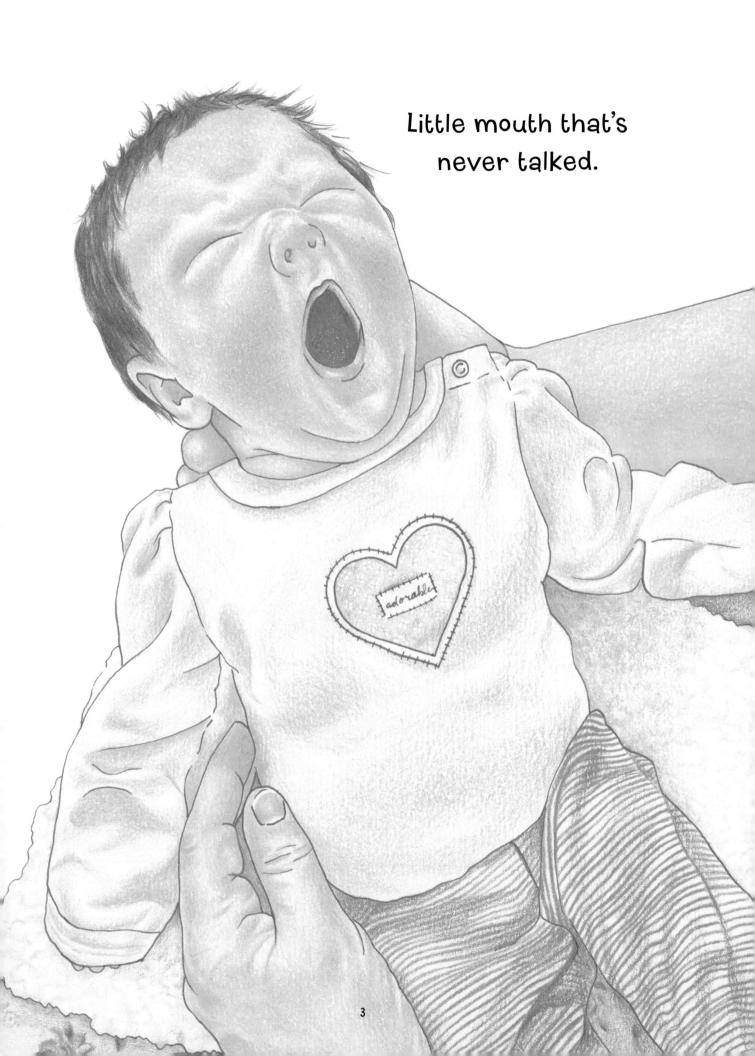

Little mouth that's
never talked.

3

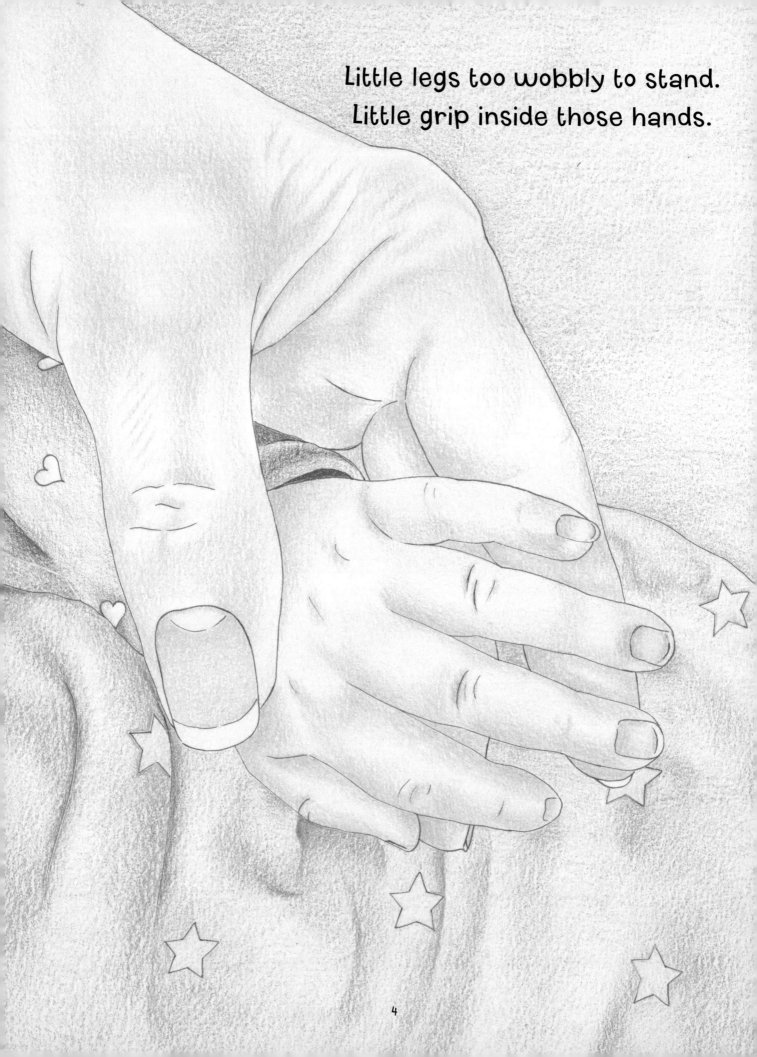

Little legs too wobbly to stand.
Little grip inside those hands.

4

What do you think?
What do you feel?

As you look
at us with
those eyes.

What do you hear?
As we speak your name.
And you listen to us
with those little ears.

We can only imagine what it is like to come from the hands of God. To be shipped from a place called heaven to a place for now we call home. Little eyes that see. Little ears that hear.

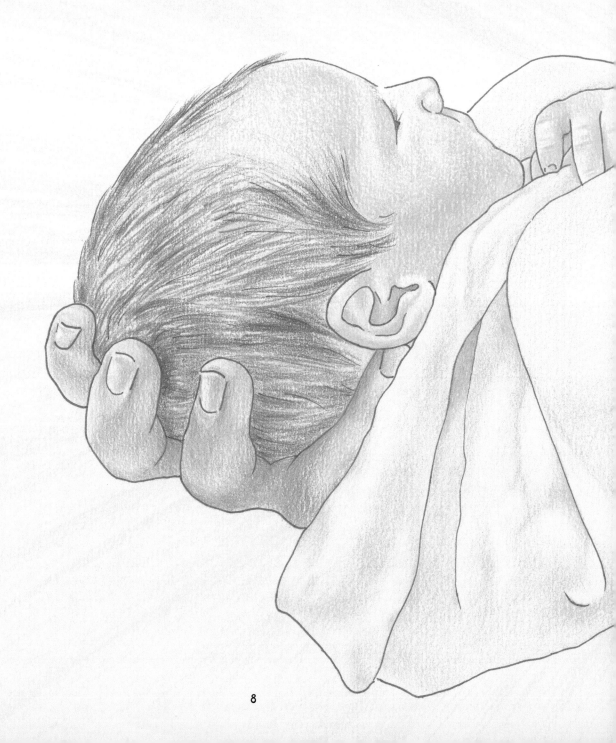

A little heart that beats. A little face that can cheer anyone of us that feels empty, lonely or sad.

You say nothing. But, we look and we see brightness, joy and sometimes tears.

Do you grin because
we are silly?
Do you grin because
we are in awe?

12

We tickle your feet.
We kiss your toes.
Such a sweet face.
Such a little nose.

Do we ever stop smiling as we look at your face?

Do you ever laugh and do you ever think?
Who are these people? Where am I now?

You are a gift! You are a
treasure! Our love for you,
can never be measured.

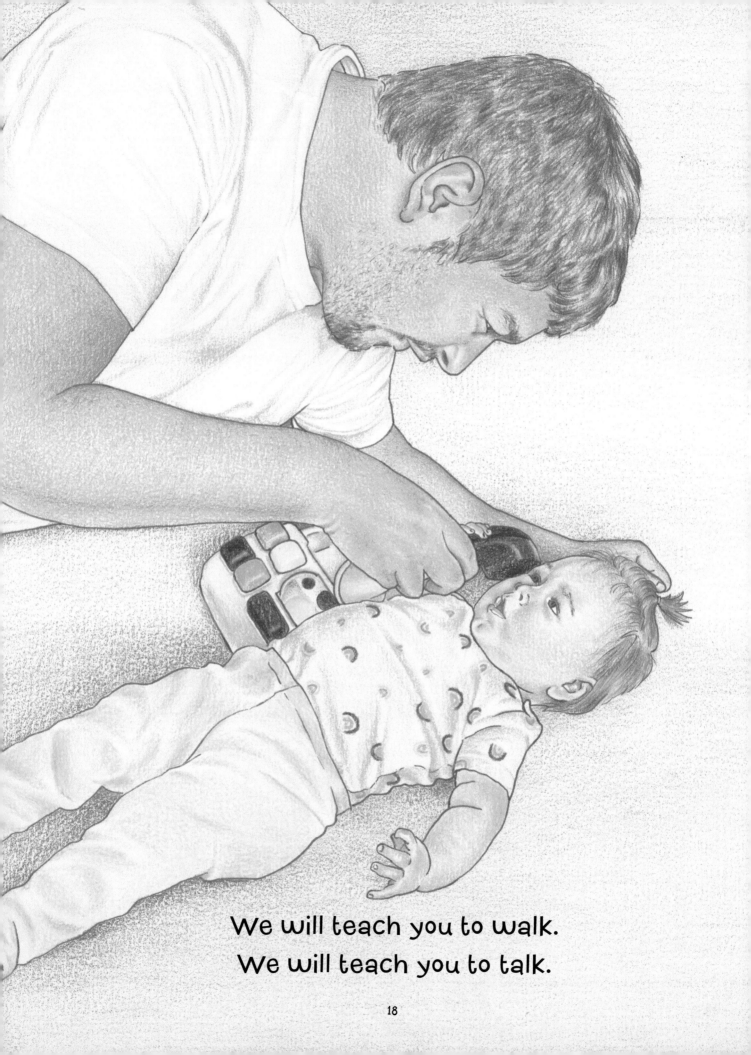

We will teach you to walk.
We will teach you to talk.

Your legs will strengthen. Your hands and arms
will squeeze us tight. And you will be amazing!

Your eyes will see the good and bad.
Your ears will listen and hear the truth.

That night, Jesus' disciples were in a locked room. Suddenly, Jesus was there. He was alive!

21

Your heart will not only beat for life, but it will also beat with emotions of love, joy and peace.

22

Do not let this world steal your joy. It
will try every day to take the happiness
God has blessed you with.

So, for now little feet that's never walked.

And a little mouth that's never talked.

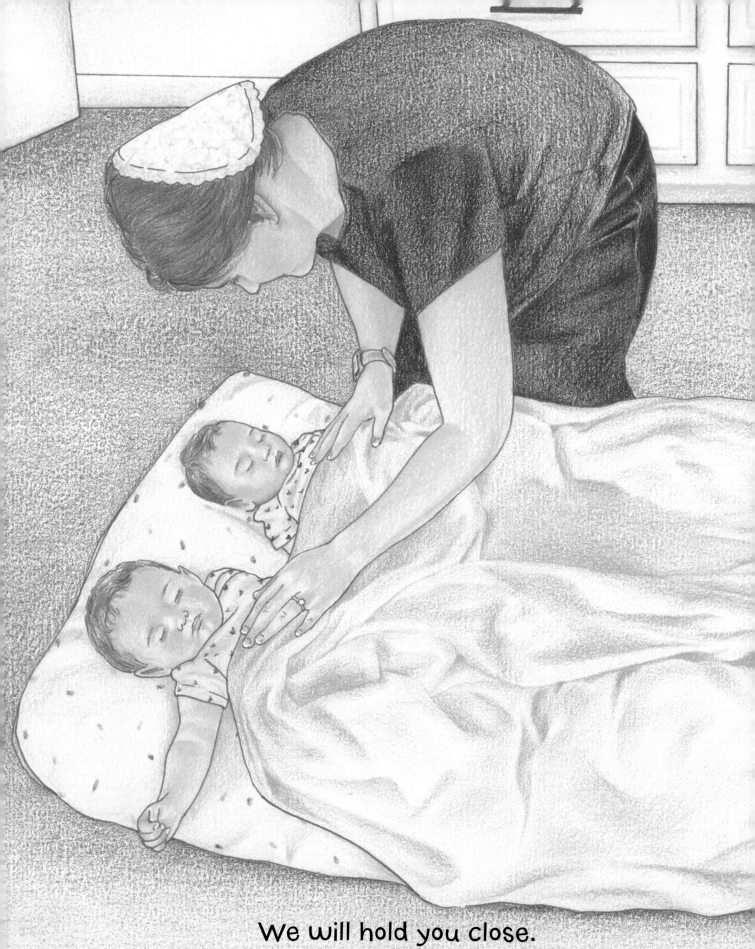

We will hold you close.
We will kneel at your bed.

We will do all we can to protect
that little heart of yours.

And you will do great
things in His name.

Printed in the United States
by Baker & Taylor Publisher Services